Biblereading
WITH YOUR KIDS

a simple guide for every father

JON NIELSON

matthiasmedia

SYDNEY · YOUNGSTOWN

Bible Reading with Your Kids

Matthias Media
(St Matthias Press Ltd ACN 067 558 365)
Email: info@matthiasmedia.com.au
Internet: www.matthiasmedia.com.au
Please visit our website for current postal and telephone contact information.

Matthias Media (USA)
Email: sales@matthiasmedia.com
Internet: www.matthiasmedia.com
Please visit our website for current postal and telephone contact information.

ISBN 978 1 922206 22 0

Cover design and typesetting by Lankshear Design.

Contents

For my parents, Niel and Kathleen, who read and taught God's word to me. I am forever grateful.

And for David Helm, who leads his family and his church according to God's good word.

Introduction

In 2011, Matthias Media published *One-to-One Bible Reading* by David Helm. I was working for David as he was writing this book, serving as the Director of Training for the Charles Simeon Trust in Chicago (an organization focused on equipping and training pastors in biblical exposition). I had a front-row seat to the formation of that book, and saw the way that a simple passion for reading the Bible one-to-one in the context of the local church had gripped David's heart. This was all taking place in his congregation long before he began to design this simple and practical manual for Christians.

But there was another aspect of David's commitment to Bible reading that gripped and shaped me during those years of service under his leadership (he was my pastor, as well as my boss). It was the way that he consistently, clearly and carefully read and explained the Bible every night over dinner to his five children. In 2007-2008, as I dated my now-wife, became engaged, and prepared for marriage, the Helm family regularly invited us into their home for dinner. We would 'sit in' on normal week-night family dinners, after which the Scriptures would be opened, the word read, and the passages discussed. The discussions were sometimes serious and often full of laughter, as well as humorous insights from the kids. Most of all, the discussions were always fully participatory—David's children were engaged with God's word! The simplicity and profundity of these after-dinner times in God's word have influenced me to this day, as I now am raising three young children of my own. I want them to know Jesus, by hearing and believing God's word. I'm forever grateful for David's example to me during those years around his table.

So, when Matthias Media approached me about writing a follow-up book to David's *One-to-One Bible Reading*—a book that would be focused on helping fathers read the Bible with their children—I jumped at the opportunity. This was not least because of my relationship with David, and the significant impact of his example to me. But it was also because I'm now working hard at figuring out how to do this well with my own kids.

Christian fathers, this book is for you. Please receive this from a dad of young kids who does not claim to have yet 'arrived' in this discipline, but has become only more and more convinced of the foundational importance of exposing our kids daily to the powerful word of God. Is there any more fundamental and important calling that we have as fathers? This is about pointing them to the only Saviour and Lord, by the surest means that God himself has provided for us.

This book is a simple, practical guide for reading God's word with your children. I offer this book to you humbly, praying that it will help you in this most important endeavour.

Jon Nielson

Part I
Why and how

VERY FEW PEOPLE WOULD disagree that exercise is good for us, and that we should exercise regularly. Yet many people who'd agree with this statement would still fail to actually *do* regular physical exercise. For many people in need of more exercise, it takes something somewhat drastic—a foreboding word from a doctor, a surprising number on a scale, a disheartening lack of 'fit' from a familiar pair of pants—to jerk them into a realization that regular physical exercise *must* become part of their life.

I think it's often like that when it comes to the subject of this little book. Very few fathers in local churches today would disagree with the statement: "Fathers should read the Bible with their children". That sounds like a very good thing, and a very godly commitment. Why, then, do so few Christian fathers seem to actually do this with regularity?

I would argue this is the case for two main reasons. First, Christian fathers have not yet been fully convinced that reading the Bible with their children *must* be done. Second, Christian fathers do not yet fully know *how* to read the Bible with their children as they grow. So it's the 'why and how' of this important task that I'll address in this first part of the book. In part II, I'll move on to give some very practical examples of what this can actually look like, based on my own experience of reading the Bible with young kids.

1 Theological foundations

A Christian leader once wrote:

> The education of children for God is the most important business done on earth... To it all politics, all war, all literature, all money-making, ought to be subordinated; and every parent especially ought to feel, every hour of the day, that, next to making [their] own calling and election sure, this is the end for which [they are] kept alive by God—this is [their] task on earth.[1]

1 RL Dabney, *Discussions of Robert Lewis Dabney,* vol. 1, Sprinkle Publications, Harrisonburg, VA, 1994 (originally published 1892), pp. 676-677.

I really think most truly Christian fathers, who genuinely know and worship Jesus Christ, honestly do believe those words. If questioned about what is most important to them in all the world concerning their children, they would answer something along the lines of: "That they love Jesus and live faithfully for God". The question for this first section of the book is... by what means will this happen? That is, what is the best and surest way that we, as fathers, can "educate children for God", as the quotation above urges? My conviction, which I believe to be the clear teaching of Scripture, is that the surest path to salvation is steady and consistent exposure to the powerful word of God. To arrive at this conviction, we may need to be reminded about what a right view of the Bible actually looks like. What really is the Bible? What does God promise that it can—and will—do in the lives of our children?

First, the Bible truly is the *living word of God.* The apostle Paul declares that all Scripture is "breathed out by God" (2 Tim 3:16). The apostle Peter asserts that the prophets of old spoke and wrote as they were "carried along by the Holy Spirit" (2 Pet 1:21). He also identifies the writings of Paul as synonymous with Old Testament Scripture (2 Pet 3:16). What do these affirmations about Scripture mean for the way we read it, study it, receive it, and apply it? It means that we approach God's word—the Bible—in a *fundamentally different* way from any other piece of literature we have ever before held in our hands.[2] The Bible is different from the writings of Plato, Aristotle, Homer, or Shakespeare. The Bible is different even from books *about* God written by brilliant theologians. Why? Because the Bible, most basically, is *God speaking*. It is so true that the Bible is God's living word that we can say, very confidently, that where the Bible speaks, God speaks.

It's this conviction that will fuel our desire to put our children in contact with Scripture very regularly. They have a Creator—a God who made them, designed them, and who loves them dearly. And, he's a Creator who longs to speak to them. It's our responsibility to allow our children to begin hearing from their Maker from the earliest of ages. When we begin to really understand the Bible as the *living word of God,* we become enthusiastically committed to helping our children listen to it!

Second, the Bible is the *authoritative word of God.* Hopefully, as we raise our young children, we are helping them understand the structure of authority in the family. We are teaching them that one of the most immediate ways they live well is by submitting to our authority as their parents. They are called to obey us—to listen to our words, and abide by our instructions. Yet, there is an even greater authority to which they—and we—are called to submit: the authority of the Creator God and his word to

2 At the same time, we also need to recognize that we come to the Bible using many of the same reading skills with which we approach any piece of literature—skills which our young children may not have acquired at all yet or are only just beginning to learn and practise. I'll have more to say about this later.

us. So we read the Bible to our children with a different tone, posture, and approach from that which we bring to any other children's story or picture book. We help them understand that we, as adults, sit under the authority of this word, just as they do. The words of this book define our lives just as they should define theirs.

Understanding the authority of God's word is part of what I sometimes call the 'pre-gospel'. Our children need to grasp this, even before they repent of sin and put their faith personally in Jesus Christ. What is this pre-gospel realization? It's the acknowledgement that they are creatures made by a Creator—he is God, and we are not. Because of this, the point of our lives becomes figuring out what the God who made us wants *from* and *for* us. Learning to sit under the authority of the word is part of responding to the Creator God in this way. It involves a recognition that our Maker has spoken with authority, and our first task as creatures is to listen to him.

Third, the Bible is the *powerful word of God*. We've talked about inspiration—the fact that the Bible really is "breathed out" by God as his very word (2 Tim 3:16). But that truth leads us to this next conviction... about the *power* of that word. Remember, we serve a God who *spoke* the entire universe into existence; his word has intrinsic creative and redemptive power. God's word is effective and powerful, unlike any of the words spoken by mere humans!

This means that his word—the Bible—is unlike any other piece of literature in *what it can accomplish* in the lives of those who read, listen to, understand and believe it. This is what the author of Hebrews tells us about God's word:

> For the word of God is living and active, sharper than any two-edged sword, piercing to the division of soul and of spirit, of joints and of marrow, and discerning the thoughts and intentions of the heart. (Heb 4:12)

God's word is alive... and it is also "active"! Paul, too, writes of the effective power of God's word to actually *get things done* in the lives of people who expose themselves to it. He tells Timothy that "Scripture is breathed out by God and profitable for teaching, for reproof, for correction, and for training in righteousness, that the man of God may be complete, equipped for every good work" (2 Tim 3:16-17). God's word, according to Paul, is not only effective for bringing people to faith in Jesus, it is also the chosen and powerful tool of God for "teaching", spiritual "training", and even for causing believers to be "complete" in their faith—a state of being fully equipped for service to Jesus Christ. Clearly there is real power attributed to this book that we can hold in our hands!

Fourth, the Bible is *God's chosen method for salvation.* It is true that, in some cases, we see God using extraordinary means to draw people into a relationship with himself. The Bible gives us examples of dreams, visions, and angels—all used by God as extraordinary methods of calling people to obedience and faith. With that being said, though, the overwhelming pattern and expectation of Scripture is that exposure to God's life-giving word is the *normal, expected, and God-ordained* means of calling sinners into a saving relationship with himself. Consider just a few passages that affirm this truth:

> ...you have been born again, not of perishable seed but of imperishable, through the living and abiding word of God. (1 Pet 1:23)
>
> How then will they call on him in whom they have not believed? And how are they to believe in him of whom they have never heard? And how are they to hear without someone preaching? And how are they to preach unless they are sent? As it is written, "How beautiful are the feet of those who preach the good news!" (Rom 10:14-15)
>
> So faith comes from hearing, and hearing through the word of Christ. (Rom 10:17)
>
> ...and how from childhood you have been acquainted with the sacred writings, which are able to make you wise for salvation through faith in Christ Jesus. (2 Tim 3:15)

Notice that in all of these verses, there is a clear and intentional link between God's word (the preaching of it, knowledge of it, etc.) and salvation. God's word is his regular and usual chosen means for bringing sinners to salvation, as his Spirit uses it to awaken dead hearts and souls and bring them to faith in Jesus. God's *word* is God's *way*. He delights to speak to people—from the earliest of ages—and invite them into a relationship with himself!

There's one more matter that we need to stop and discuss together at this point. It's the absolutely necessity of adding our *prayers* to the work of reading and teaching the Bible to our children. It would be possible, I suppose, to do everything 'right' in exposing our kids to God's word, and totally miss the absolutely necessary role of God *himself* in the entire process. Why must we lead with prayer? Why is it so necessary for us to bathe our Bible reading and teaching with our children in earnest pleas to God on their behalf?

- First, because salvation is always a miracle. Remember those familiar words from Paul in 2 Corinthians 5:17-18: "Therefore, if anyone is in Christ, he is a new creation. The old has passed away; behold, the new has come. All this is *from God...*" Anyone—man, woman, or child—who responds to the truths of God's word with repentance from sin and faith in God is experiencing something that is supernatural. It is a miracle; God gives faith to sinful people so that they become completely "new". All of our teaching, Bible reading, and pleading with our children can't force them to become new creations. The best we can do is bear witness to the God who can... and earnestly ask him to do a saving work in our sons and daughters.
- Second, because God responds to our prayers. This is not a book on prayer, so we don't have time to get into the theological intricacies of how prayer works. But it's safe to say that the model we see throughout Scripture and history is of God

moving in response to the prayers of his people. Now, we must always be careful not to seek to manipulate or control God; he will work and save in *his* way, and in *his* time. Yet, there is good precedent for God answering the prayers of his people, especially when they ask for things according to his will and heart (and the conversion and faith of little children certainly falls into this category!). We pray, trusting that God hears, and that he will answer in his time, and in his way.

- Third, consistent prayer to God for our children reminds us of his prominent and fundamental role in their lives. Of course we are witnesses, teachers, models, and guides. But he alone, by the power of the Holy Spirit, can change their hearts. When we pray for our kids—along with reading the Bible to them—we remind our own hearts that we are not fundamentally responsible for their conversion. That is God's work, and so we make our earnest appeal to our Heavenly Father on their behalf—a Father who loves them far better than we ever could.

Do you really believe it?

So, the power of God's word is immense. We've looked at just a few characteristics of Scripture, which should certainly get us excited about exposing our children to its power, even as we commit every step of the way to committing our work and witness to God in prayer.

Let me stop here then and ask you: Do you believe that all of this is true about the Bible? Again, do you *really* believe these claims about God's word? Are you convicted that the Bible is God's *living word*—inspired by the Holy Spirit himself, and so closely associated with God's communication with us that we can say confidently that "where the Bible speaks, God speaks"? Do you really believe that the Bible is God's *authoritative word,* under which you must call your children to sit, even more fundamentally than they sit under your authority as their father? Do you really believe that the Bible is God's *powerful word*—able to grip the hearts of your children and awaken them to faith in Christ Jesus by the power of God's Spirit? Do you really believe that God's word is *his chosen method*—throughout every age—of bringing people to faith and moving them on in obedience? If you really believe these things, then your only conclusion must be that there is no better spiritual gift to offer your children than *steady and consistent and prayer-backed exposure to this word of God.* As Christian fathers, we must do this. And we must do it well.

2 Practical foundations

So you have these basic theological convictions about what the Bible is, and about how God delights to use his word in the lives of his people. You're coming under the conviction that you *must* commit to this with your children. But before we delve further into how this can be done, let's discuss some of the *practical* reasons for reading the Bible with your kids .

First, the *fatherhood factor.* Like it or not, for both boys and girls, the spiritual engagement of their father is statistically the most influential factor in determining whether they grow up to identify as Christian and attend church regularly. This is no secret—in fact it's a well-researched fact. A 1994 study from Switzerland is perhaps the most often-referenced on this point.[3] It found that for children of parents who both attended church in Switzerland, roughly 33 per cent of them grew up to attend church regularly. When only the mother attended, that percentage plummeted to three per cent. Amazingly, for children of married parents in which *only* the father attended church regularly, the percentage of children growing up to become church attendees held steady... and even slightly *increased!* Clearly, this study gives at least some serious indications that children grow up taking their spiritual 'cues' from their fathers. Very often, as Dad goes spiritually, so go the children. What a great practical argument for Christian fathers to lead their children spiritually!

Second, the *relationship factor*. By committing to read the Bible regularly with our children early on in their lives, we are helping to lay a foundation for an ongoing relationship with them that will be founded—at least in part—on regular engagement with God's word. By God's grace, this can form the natural 'rhythm' of our conversations with them for many years to come. Our kids will see discussion about God's word as a natural and normal part of our relationship with them, rather than an awkwardly forced topic initiated irregularly by Mum and Dad.

---

3 Werner Haug and Phillipe Warner, 'The demographic characteristics of the linguistic and religious groups in Switzerland', *Population Studies*, vol. 2, no. 31, 1994. This report also appears in a book titled *The Demographic Characteristics of National Minorities in Certain European States*, ed. Werner Haug, Council of Europe Directorate General III, Social Cohesion, Strasbourg, January 2000.

We've already begun to see the fruit of this with our kids. Yes, we talk about the Bible when we read it together and discuss it before bed. But questions about God, salvation, sin, and Scripture have often naturally come up in the course of our day as well. Our kids have begun to see conversation about the things of God as a normal and joyful part of their relationship with us. Now, of course we know there will be difficult times in our relationship with our kids—especially as they enter the teenage years. But our hope is that this foundation-laying commitment to reading and discussing the Bible with them will bear fruit many years down the road, as we seek to bring gospel truths to bear in every struggle, disagreement, discipline, and conversation.

Third, the *capacity factor.* By this, I'm referring to the surprising capacity of our children to begin grasping the major themes and theological teachings of Scripture from an early age. I say "major themes" and "theological teachings" specifically; our children can grasp these in addition to the stories of Scripture (which are usually the only things that we credit them with being able to understand).

Just the other night, I was reading Genesis 3 with my 5-year-old and 3-year-old daughters before bed. As is my habit, I finished the brief reading and asked them a few follow-up questions to gauge how well they had understood the story (I was more concerned with their comprehension of the words of God to Eve and to the serpent than of the narrative itself, which I knew they had heard before many times). My 5-year-old, whom I thought had been zoning out a bit, responded right away when I asked her to explain God's words to Eve. "Dad", she said, "I think that God was telling Eve that one of her children would grow up to cut off Satan's head". Not completely accurate, but surprisingly close! And so, we proceeded to have a general introduction to the 'first gospel', or 'protoevangelion' as the theologians call it, which God gives to his people in Genesis 3:15. We spent time talking about the grace and love of God—that he would offer a word of good news, even after Adam and Eve had just disobeyed his direct command. We talked and prayed to Jesus—the one whom God was promising to send for the sake of sinners.

Now, just to be clear, I didn't use the word, 'protoevangelion', with my children, in the midst of that discussion, and neither should you! But the concept—that God promised to one day kill Satan—was clear to my kids through the simple reading of the word. They were able to grasp more than I might have assumed they could. I know they didn't get everything right (my daughter said that the serpent's head would get "cut off", rather than "crushed"). Still, they were able to pick up themes and truths from God's word as I read it aloud to them and asked them questions.

So here's my point: our kids can pick up more than *just* the stories, even from an early age. They can begin to grasp the arc of redemptive history, the concept of the grace of God, and the reality of sin and judgement. And they can pick those themes up through *hearing the Bible read to them*. We need to recognize their capacity for this! Now, of course, the Bible will need some explanation because some of the vocabulary and concepts will be new to our children. So the process is going to look different for an 8-year-old than for a 3-year-old, and there are obviously age-appropriate (and inappropriate) ways to engage with our children about Scripture. But we'll probably find they surprise us along the way with their comprehension and internalization of God's word! So we want to be optimistic and hopeful about our kids' ability to pick up the realities of God, sin, and salvation through Jesus.[4]

Fourth, the *relevance factor*. Scripture is not just "breathed out by God and profitable" (2 Tim 3:16) for adults. It is extremely relevant and applicable to the lives of children too. Children get anxious; the Bible helps them to see that God is a loving Father who is in control of their world and urges them to pray (Phil 4:6). Children are growing up in a world confused about gender and sexuality; the Bible shows them God's good created order and intention for us. Children are sinful in their behaviours at times; the Bible calls them out on that, tells them they need to repent and live God's way, and assures them of God's willingness to forgive through Christ. Let there be no doubt—reading the Bible is very relevant to our kids' lives and enables them to begin responding and relating to God in healthy ways even at a young age.

4 Having said that, at times they can also surprise us with their misunderstandings too. So as we'll discuss later, we need to keep checking in with them and asking them questions.

Summary

So, fathers, there are four practical (although still spiritual) reasons for giving yourself to this Bible-reading commitment with your children. They will take their spiritual cues from you; that's the *fatherhood factor*. You can establish conversation about God's word as a regular and normal aspect of your interaction with them; that's the *relationship factor*. You can help your children begin to understand the deep theological truths of the Bible from very early ages; that's the *capacity factor*. Finally, the Bible speaks to your children at their own stage of life; that's the *relevance factor*.

Hopefully, you've been convinced (or perhaps you already were!) that spending intentional time with your kids in God's word is an absolutely essential part of your role as a father. The exposure of your kids to the power of God's word—in conjunction with your prayers, and the work of the Holy Spirit in their hearts—is truly sufficient to change them, form them, and direct them to faith in Jesus Christ that lasts.

3 How should I approach this?

So now we turn to the more practical and hands-on part of this book. We want to examine in a little more detail *how* we can actually read the Bible in an effective way with our children. In chapter 4, I'll set out eight practical tips for doing this. But before we get to that, we'll need to reflect a little bit on our approach to this task as Christian fathers. We'll also need to think quite a bit about where each of our children are at, taking into account their age and developmental stage, as we engage them in God's word.

As Christian fathers

The reality is that all of us dads come to this job of reading and teaching the Bible to our kids from different starting points. You may have only recently come to faith in Christ yourself, and are pretty much as unaware of the content of the Bible as your kids are. Or at the other end of the spectrum, you might have been a Christian for many years, read the Bible cover to cover multiple times, and even had some formal theological education. Perhaps, like me, you have the privilege of teaching the Bible to people as a full-time job, so you are very comfortable in opening up the Bible and explaining it—it's what you do more than just about anything else each week.

But the key thing to remember is this: the responsibility to teach your kids God's word is given to you regardless of how ill-equipped or how well-equipped you feel for the task. And anyone can do it. In fact, the New Testament's expectation is that *all* Christians will be involved in teaching and encouraging each other with the word of Christ (Col 3:16)—it's not something you opt out of because you don't think you're qualified.

If you are more down the 'I feel ill-equipped' end of the spectrum, I want to encourage you to just get in and have a go. Don't put it off until you feel ready; just get started. Sure, you may need to rely a bit more on your preparation and the use of helpful resources than some other dads. But by now I hope I have persuaded you that it is *certainly* worth investing time and effort into reading the Bible to your kids.

One of the habits you could get into is to read with your children the parts of the Bible you are reading in your own personal Bible reading time the day or two before. Just add an extra step to the end of your own

Bible reading process: ask yourself "How will I explain these verses to my kids tomorrow?" What are the tricky words and ideas that you will need to simplify and clarify? (By the way, I'm convinced that taking this extra step will not only help your kids, but also help you to grapple with what God is saying in his word at a much deeper level and get more out of it.)

With our children

If you're anything like me, the task of reading and studying the Bible with young children hasn't always come easily—and it's not even necessarily because of anything to do with the Bible. Kids can be fidgety, restless, and distracted... not to mention the fact that there are more media options than ever with which to entertain them.[5] How do we engage with our kids around Scripture—especially in the age of smartphones, games on tablets, and television shows that pop up at the press of a button?

Just to be clear, this book is not going to focus too much on children who are babies and very young toddlers (ages 1-2). To be sure, I think the practice of reading Scripture to children at those ages is valuable. I believe strongly that reading the Bible, singing hymns,

5 I'm also conscious that it can be even tougher for some kids who have issues with things like Attention Deficit Hyperactivity Disorder (ADHD). Dealing with that scenario is beyond the scope of this book, but I encourage you to get professional help with it and to talk honestly with other Christian parents who have kids who struggle with ADHD.

and praying aloud even to our babies can be a wonderful step toward acquainting them with those practices from their earliest ages. In fact, God may even use this in ways we don't quite understand. But for the purpose of this part of the book, I'm going to be focusing mainly on reading the Bible with children who can engage with it verbally at some level—beginning probably at age 3 or so, depending on the child. In other words, we're talking about children who can begin to grasp the truths being taught in the Bible, and respond to simple questions that gauge their comprehension.

At the older end of the spectrum, this book is not going to focus on children too much older than age 12. Somewhere around that age, our children should be transitioning to some practice of personal devotions (Bible reading and prayer), and engagement in church and youth group at a bit more of an 'adult' level. Of course, we don't ever stop caring for our children spiritually. And our role as parents during our kids' teenage years becomes more and more significant as they increasingly face the issues of the world. But we do move into a phase that involves less input from us in directing their Bible reading, as we encourage them to engage with God's word for themselves.

So the primary focus of this little book is to help us as parents engage with our children during those formative, 'elementary' years—ages 3-12.

With this age range in mind, let me just add that the tips for reading the Bible with our children set out in chapter 4 are generally applicable for all ages within that range (3-12). Obviously some adjustments will be required depending on the age of your child. These age adjustments should be fairly intuitive to you as parents—you most likely do it all the time in day-to-day interactions with your kids. But if it doesn't feel all that intuitive, let me give you three quick principles for how to approach it.

The **first** principle is to think about how you would talk to someone who has only just started learning English as their second language. And, no, it doesn't actually help that person if you just talk *louder*! But it *does* help if you slow down your speech a bit, because that person will have to think more carefully about each word as you say it. You will also think carefully about the words you use, choosing simpler, more common words they are more likely to have learned. Do the same with kids.

The **second** principle is to think about how you learn mathematics. This principle makes up for the partial inadequacy of the first principle, because it is actually a mistake to think that young kids are just the same as adults who are learning English. Children are not adults in their capacity to think—their brains are still developing, and this is particularly true in the area of abstract and concrete thinking. (When you use metaphors, similes, and parables, you are definitely in the realm of the abstract.)

So, think about how kids learn mathematics.

When they are toddlers they will most likely learn their numbers, and how to say "one, two, three... nine, ten". At this early stage, they are just words to them—words they have learned to say in a standard sequence.

In the next step of learning, children will understand that those words represent quantities. So your child can look at two apples and say "there are two apples". It's still a pretty concrete concept though: there are two physical objects they can point to. But later they can begin to think more abstractly and understand that 'two' is a concept that can apply to anything, not just apples, and so they start to understand that 1+1=2. Later still, they get even more abstract in their thinking as the numbers themselves are symbolized with letters and they begin learning algebra (i.e. that x+y=z).

Start talking to a 3-year-old about x and y adding up to z and they may well nod sagely, but unless you have an amazing prodigy, the synapses will definitely not be firing. They are not going to understand.

So as you read the Bible, train yourself to spot abstract concepts and where possible try to explain them in concrete terms to children who are still at that stage.

The **third** principle is also another outworking of the difference between adults and children, and it relates to the breadth of their personal experience. There are lots of seemingly straightforward descriptions in the Bible that still might need some extra explanation for our kids. For example, when the Gospels talk about Jesus calming a storm (Matt 8:23-27; Mark 4:35-41), you know as an adult what that means and you can imagine the scene. But has your 3-year-old ever seen a storm? Do they know what that is? And have they seen roaring waves? Similarly, when Jesus calls fishermen as his first disciples, and they immediately leave their nets and follow him (Matt 4:18-22), *you* can picture the scene. But does your child know what a fisherman does? And what "nets" are for? If not, you might have to explain these kinds of things by referring to other objects and events that they know and have experienced.

For your help, in part II I'll offer some brief guidelines for working toward Bible reading with younger children (ages 3-6), before giving some longer examples of what Bible reading times can look like for slightly older children (ages 7-12).

Let me make one more point absolutely clear: as we move into these eight practical tips, I want to stress that I am talking about reading the *actual words of Scripture* to your children. I'm not talking about children's Bibles, although those can be helpful at various points—for example, we've loved using David Helm's *Big Picture Story Bible* (published by Crossway). I'm also not talking about merely telling your children Bible stories in your own words, although that can certainly be a wonderful practice as well. What I want to do is to help you engage your children with the actual text of Scripture—reading the words of the Bible to them directly, and leading them toward a growing engagement with God's word itself. That is the focus of this book, and it grows out of the core conviction that permeated the first chapter—that it is *intelligible exposure* to God's word, empowered by God's Holy Spirit and fuelled by our prayers, that brings lasting change, worship, and discipleship in Jesus to our kids.

With all of this now said, let's dive into the eight tips! *How* do we dig into the Bible with our children?

4 8 practical tips

THESE ARE A FEW PRACTICES that my wife and I have found to be extremely helpful (at the time of the writing of this book, my children are aged 5, 3, and almost 2).

1. Pick a regular time and place for Bible reading

In general, children tend to love some kind of routine—a special, regular, and anticipated time with Mum and/or Dad that is associated with a particular activity. Because of this, sporadic and somewhat 'random' Bible reading time may not engage your children in the same way that a regular, planned, and prioritized 'special' time will. In our home, we've chosen (as many of you probably will) the 'before-bed' chunk of time for our Bible reading. Our two older children know that, in the 15-20 minutes before bed, we're going to gather in their room to read a Bible passage, discuss it together, and pray. They've come to look forward to it; it's as regular and natural a process as brushing their teeth, and I think it probably even helps them sleep better, as many before-bed routines seem to do.

If you're just getting started, and haven't yet decided on a regular time and place for Bible reading, I would encourage you to involve your children in this choice. Maybe bedtime is the logical choice. But maybe (especially if you're kids are slightly older) the time around the dinner table directly after eating is the better time. The dinner hour can often be a great time for family connection: conversations about the day, laughter, and a time for reflection. This can lead naturally into a time of Bible reading, discussion, and prayer. Make it clear to your kids that you're going to pick a regular time to engage with them about God's word, and see what they think!

2. Read short chunks of Scripture

For some of us, we'll have to guard against being overly ambitious as we start this practice! We believe in the power of God's word, and we rightly want our children to be exposed to as much of it as possible. But, as you can imagine, reading two full chapters from Genesis each night could well cause a 5-year-old's eyes to glaze over! A straight reading of such a large chunk of the Old Testament is likely to be too much.

So as you begin, let me encourage you to select manageable passages from Scripture, based on an honest assessment of your children's developmental stage.

The key is not to rush it, and to think ahead of time about the right chunks to focus on each day. In the book of Genesis, for example, we moved at the rate of approximately one chapter per day, but there were some chapters that we decided to either skip, or summarize briefly as a kid-friendly version. (For example, see chapter 8 for my 'G-rated' summary of Genesis 38!) In general, you want to stick to chunks of the Bible each day that contain one main point, and one main application, on which you can focus together as a family. Genesis 3 works well as an example of this. You read the story of the temptation of Eve by Satan, and then the disobedience of both Adam and Eve, followed by God's response to their sin. That's a big enough chunk to engage children as a full story, but small enough to have some key points to hone in on together (God's word, obedience, sin, results of sin, etc.). It's helpful to plan a few days ahead, choosing logical and manageable sections of Scripture to read and discuss each day, and thinking about how you will simplify words and explain some of those abstract concepts (obedience, sin, etc.).

3. Where possible, pick a literal Bible translation

Here we come to a little more nuanced and complicated point. Parents often ask about the best Bible translation to use with young children—and the answers from Christian leaders and other Christian parents are varied. Some insist on reading the actual words of Scripture to children from the youngest of ages. Some parents have decided to make use of paraphrases. Others are still reading children's story Bibles to their children aged 8, 9, and even 10 and 11. What do we do about the difficulty in comprehension that can exist for, say, a 6-year-old who is listening to the Bible read from an adult translation?

What I want to propose here is that you, as parents, should actually consider using an 'essentially literal' Bible translation when reading Scripture to older children. There is a spectrum of Bible translation philosophies and approaches, and the 'essentially literal' approach gives a word for word translation of each passage from the Greek (New Testament) and Hebrew (Old Testament) Scriptures. Translations that fall in this category include the English Standard Version (ESV), Revised Standard Version (RSV), and New American Standard Version (NASB). This is in contrast to a 'dynamic equivalent' approach, which takes more of a 'phrase by phrase' or 'idea by idea' approach to translation. Translations that fall in this category include the New International Version (NIV), Today's New International Version (TNIV), New International Reader's Version (NIrV) and the New Living Translation (NLT). Further down the spectrum, you get to paraphrases of the Bible, which would include versions like Eugene Peterson's *The Message* (published by NavPress). Pass that, and you come to children's Bibles, which are usually not claiming to be translations at all, or even paraphrases, of Scripture—they are usually summaries of key Bible stories and teachings.

We've already talked about the importance of intelligible exposure to the *actual* words of God. But there's also another reason why I suggest you use an 'essentially literal' translation when reading the Bible to your kids. It's my conviction that doing so enables (and perhaps requires!) you to do the work of pastoring your family, as you read the Bible, and then *interpret and apply it* to your children in the context of your home, life, and relationships. In other words, I, as a father, want to read to my children the best and most direct translation of God's word possible. Then, I want to paraphrase, interpret, and apply it myself (rather than have somebody else do it!). It's my conviction that any father or mother can learn to do this. Yes, it takes time and commitment, but it is absolutely possible. You don't need to be a professional Bible teacher to do it (although you will be helped by the sermons you listen to at church and other contact with solid Christian teaching).[6] We'll think more about what this interpretation, summary, and application can look like with your kids in chapter 8, where I'll give some examples of what this can look like in practice.

Now if you really do feel like that is beyond your capacity, I do want to emphasize that it is a whole lot better to read a simplified translation to your children than not to read the Bible to them at all. So don't let my ideal of using a literal translation prevent you from taking a good first step.

---

6 You may well find it helpful to do a basic course in Bible reading and interpretation. *Six Steps to Reading Your Bible* (Matthias Media) is a good example of one such course. David Helm's *One-to-One Bible Reading* (Matthias Media) also has some helpful material on how to read different parts of the Bible and different genres within the Bible.

4. Stop often to explain and gauge comprehension

We talked earlier about choosing manageable chunks of Scripture to read to your children each day; this is important, so that we don't overwhelm our 5-year-olds with too much Scripture and theology at once! But even if the allocated chunk for the day is just one chapter, that can still be a lot for a young child to handle if it's read all at once without stopping. So I want to highlight how incredibly important it is to stop often along the way (during the actual reading of the biblical text), to explain things, ask questions to gauge comprehension, and ensure that your kids are really following along and getting what the passage is saying. Any classroom teacher knows how essential it is to ask questions to 'check in' with their students along the way, especially during an extended lesson. The point here is the same.

I'll do this with my 5-year-old and my 3-and-a half-year-old whenever I get the sense that their minds are wandering a bit. I'll stop—sometimes mid-sentence—and say something like: "OK, what just happened right there? Can someone tell me what's going on with King Saul at this point?" Often they're eager to jump in and explain what has been happening. Or, if they've missed something, I can fill it in for them, and then they can get right back into the progression of the story or passage. It takes some work and attention to keep them with you, but it's important... and worth it down the road.

5. Think of age-appropriate questions for follow-up discussion

I must say, this aspect of Bible reading with my kids has quickly become their favourite part of our nightly time together in God's word! I've started the practice of thinking up a few basic questions for each of them that will help them to a) solidify their comprehension of the passage, b) connect the passage to the overall story of the Bible, and c) apply it to their own lives, and their developing relationships with God. I'll give some very specific examples of what these questions can look like in chapter 8; for now, let me just explain the importance of this step.

When you ask simple questions of your children after they've read God's word, you're doing much more than simply quizzing them to make sure they were paying attention. You are actually leading them, interactively, in a time of interpreting and applying the Bible. To put it in slightly different words, you are helping them do the work of Bible study, and preparing them to engage with God's word directly on their own in the years to come. You begin by making sure that they've understood the story or passage. But then you intentionally move them toward seeing the passage in light of God's big plan of redemption through Jesus Christ (again, I'll give some very concrete examples of how to do this in chapter 8). Finally, you're trying to help them—night after night and day after day—to connect the truths of God's word to their daily lives, even in very simple and very practical ways. Why is this step so important? Because you're beginning to model to them how a follower of Jesus treats the Bible as the *living and active* word of God—an authoritative word that is meant to influence the way we live, think, speak, and act.

It's important to note that coming up with the right questions, and the right *kinds* of questions, for children of specific ages will sometimes take some preparation and very careful thought. Although forming age-appropriate questions can sometimes be more difficult than we think at first, remember that as parents, you are the best people to work out what kind of questions will work for your child, because you know where they're at! When we get these questions right, this last step in the your Bible reading time can really help the Scriptures click with our kids. As I mentioned before, 'question time' has become one of the highlights of my daughters' time with me at night. They beg me to ask them the first question, and love demonstrating that they've understood the passage we've read. It's also been a beautiful thing to watch my older daughter explaining to my younger daughter certain nuanced points of the story that she hasn't quite been able to grasp. She's learning to be a Bible teacher to her younger sister... praise God!

6. Connect each story/passage to Jesus

Jesus makes an amazing—even shocking—statement to the Pharisees in John 5, as they continue to struggle to believe in him as the Messiah, the Son of God. In fact, it's a statement that would be brazenly arrogant if it were said by anyone else in history... because it wouldn't be true. To the Jewish religious leaders of his day, he says this: "You search the Scriptures because you think that in them you have eternal life; and it is they that bear witness about me" (v. 39). Jesus is saying, in no uncertain terms, that the biblical Scriptures (in the context, particularly the Old Testament texts) are centred around *him*—his incarnation, his life, his teaching, his death, his resurrection—as the central climax that holds all Scripture together. He is the central figure of the Bible. The Old Testament pointed ahead to him as the great Saviour, King, Prophet, Priest and Lord, who would fulfil all of God's redemptive promises to his people for all time. What does this mean for our daily Bible reading with our kids? It means that as we try to help them understand any part of the Bible, we need to give them a sense of how that part connects to the major character, and the great climax, of the overarching story.

Now, this is obviously not the place for a fully-fledged biblical theology, or a guide on how every difficult Old Testament passage connects to Jesus Christ and the gospel. It's enough, for now, for you to become convinced that your Bible reading needs to be connected to Jesus, in some way, day in and day out. Some passages in the New Testament, of course, will connect to Jesus immediately. But it can be more difficult in the Old Testament. Some passages will point ahead to Jesus through *promises* that God makes to his people, which will ultimately be fulfilled through Jesus (think, for example, of the big promise that God makes to Abraham in Genesis 12:3 that "all the families of the earth shall be blessed" through the line of Abraham). Other passages will connect to Jesus through *patterns* of God's work in the world for his people, which whet our appetite for the coming of Jesus, and show us how he delights to bring salvation (consider the events of 1 Samuel 16 and 17, where God sets a pattern of setting his anointing on a chosen deliverer for his people, and then empowers that 'saviour' to do battle on behalf of his people against their enemies). Still other passages present a particular *person* who serves as a 'type' of Christ in some way (Moses, for example, serves as a kind of prophet and mediator for God's people and prefigures Jesus as the ultimate Prophet and Mediator). Other passages, in the prophetic books for example, give us very direct *predictions* about what God's final and ultimate saving work in the world is going to look like. (Isaiah, for example, speaks in chapter 53 of the role of a 'suffering servant' who will one day come to bear the sins of God's people on himself.)

We could go on, but hopefully you get the picture! Your job, as a parent, will be to get better and better at helping your kids put the Bible together as one big story of God's saving work in the world, centred on the coming and work of Jesus, his Son.[7]

7 There are some good books and resources that can help you put the big picture together yourself. Graeme Goldsworthy's *Gospel and Kingdom* (Paternoster Press) and Vaughn Roberts' *God's Big Picture: Tracing the Storyline of the Bible* (Inter-Varsity Press) are excellent books. *Full of Promise* (Matthias Media) is a Bible study by Bryson Smith and Phil Campbell which takes you through the Bible story's key landmarks in eight studies, and *The Bible Overview* (Matthias Media) offers an excellent visual presentation of the Bible's overarching story (that actually works well with kids as well as adults).

7. Let the Bible reading guide you to a time of prayer

Listening to kids who are learning to pray can be humorous. If your kids are anything like mine, their prayers sometimes can be hilarious in their simplicity... and self-focus! We've heard prayers in our home for dogs, movies, imaginary people, and, of course, much-coveted toys. But if we're honest, even as adults we are not immune to these kinds of self-centred prayers. We also can struggle with a mundane routine of prayer—finding ourselves repeating often-used phrases again and again. We can very easily resort to praying only for our needs and wants, rather than spending time in praise and adoration of God, and asking for his Spirit's work in the lives of others. One way to grow in our prayer lives is to more *intentionally connect our prayers with our daily reading and study of God's word*. We can, in other words, 'talk back' to God daily, based on the ways he is speaking to us through the Scriptures.

In our prayer time with our children, we have the opportunity to model the impulse of 'talking back' to God about his word, allowing the Scriptures to dictate and guide the way we respond to our Heavenly Father in prayer. We can help guide them away from merely 'recited' prayers ("God, thank you for this day", "God, please bless Mum and Dad", "God, help me to have a good sleep", etc.) toward prayers that are uniquely connected to the lessons they are learning each day from Scripture.

This practice (which we will demonstrate more specifically in chapter 8) will begin to do a few things in the hearts and minds of our children. First, it will help them think about prayer as more than a routine—more than something we just do mechanically at the end of the day and before meals. It will help them think about prayer as 'alive'—a conversation with God that is informed by the way his word is teaching us and shaping our lives. Second, it will begin to change their view of the Bible; no longer will it be like any other storybook, but rather a story that is still being told by a living God and Father. In other words, they see that they can actually 'talk back' to the Storyteller himself, responding to a God who is alive, listening, and responsive to our prayers. Third, it will help reinforce the interpretation and application of the Bible passages. Preparing our kids for prayer, based on the passage we've just read, gives us an opportunity to ask them to consider: "What can we ask God to help us with, based on this story?", "What do you think God wanted from his people in this passage?", "What does that tell us about how we should talk to him now?" Taking the main points and applications from Scripture directly into a time of prayer can powerfully reinforce what our children are learning from God's word each day.

8. Be willing to do it badly

One frequently used phrase around our house is this one: "If a thing is worth doing, it's worth doing badly"![8]

8 This phrase was coined by GK Chesterton in *What's Wrong With the World?*, Dodd, Mead, and Company, New York, 1910, p. 320.

Of course, this is a bit of a tongue-in-cheek response to another oft-quoted proverb: "If a thing is worth doing, it's worth doing well". I like this change, though, because it fits with the fact that we are so often called to do very important, valuable things, regardless of how *well* we can do them—and even if we can't do them perfectly (or even very well at all) at the outset. So many things, including Bible reading, are worth doing poorly... at least at the beginning. This is an exhortation that I give to college students who are just getting into personal devotions for the first time in their lives. I encourage them to start—no matter what their starting point looks like. Even if it's reading just a few verses a day, and that's an increase from zero verses a day, then we're moving in the right direction!

So if you're beginning a consistent pattern of reading the Bible with your children, be willing to do it poorly at the outset. Set reasonable expectations; don't expect everything just to click into place overnight. There may be dull moments. Your kids may even be resistant to this new routine at first. Stick with it, though, and I truly believe you will find this to be a key part of their growth in Jesus... as well as the growth of your spiritual relationship with them and role in their lives.

Dads, you really can do this. Be willing to begin. Be willing to do it badly at the outset. But, give yourself to the discipline of reading the Bible to your children daily, explaining it to them, asking them questions, and leading them in prayer to God about what he is teaching you together through his word.

5 A final encouragement

Before I offer a final exhortation to *get going with this* with your children, I want to give you one more word of encouragement about what this discipline of Bible reading will do in *your* heart and life as a parent. Let me offer three potential benefits that you will enjoy, as you give yourself to this.

First, you will see your own understanding of the Bible grow and develop as you read it and explain it to your children. Any good teacher, in any particular subject, will tell you that one good test of true comprehension of a complex concept is whether or not you could explain it with clarity to a young child. While it will be challenging to read the Bible and explain it with clarity to, for example, your 8-year-old, it will force *you* to work hard to comprehend biblical stories, ideas, and teachings with pinpoint clarity. By God's grace, my conviction is that this forces us to work even harder in our own understanding of God's word. This will be good for our hearts and minds!

Second, you will see yourself develop as a teacher of God's word. While some of us may never become public preachers of the Bible from the pulpit, *all* of us are to be involved in word ministry in the context of the body of Christ, the local church (see Colossians 3:16, for example, where Paul calls ordinary Christians to "teach" and "admonish" one another according to the word of Christ). Your daily commitment to reading the Bible with your children, and explaining it to them with clarity along the way, will equip you to steadily grow in your ability to do word ministry with adults too—for example, in your church small group and other social settings. As you start to do more 'God talk' with your kids and articulate gospel truths aloud with them, you may even find that you're able to do personal evangelism with more confidence, clarity, winsomeness, and ease!

Third, with all my heart, I believe that you will find your love for your children growing through this discipline, and your relationship with them being enriched and strengthened. You will enjoy sweet conversations with them about the things of God, as they form questions, wrestle through theological truths, and discover new and beautiful things about God, his grace, and his glorious redemption of sinners. This will be good for your heart, as you see a new dimension of spiritual friendship opening up between you and your children, which can continue to grow and flourish as they get older.

• • •

NOW, IT'S TIME TO BEGIN. Let me encourage you to go for it! Begin right now. Measure your expectations, and allow yourself grace. There will be some tough times; young kids can have trouble focusing, and we've certainly had our nights when Bible reading times have been a struggle! But... it's worth it. Expose your kids to God's word daily, and commit them to him in prayer, trusting him to open their hearts to his gospel by the power of the Holy Spirit.

Part II
What this can look like

AS WE BEGIN THIS SECTION, our goal will now be to get even more practical in showing you what Bible reading with our children can actually *look like*, and even *sound like*.

In chapter 7 I've provided three **sample Bible reading plans**—the actual passages and verses that you could read with your children night by night to move through an entire book of the Bible together over a few weeks.

In chapter 8 I give three **sample Bible reading sessions**. These take the form of a 'script' of things that might be spoken as you lead your child in their devotional time. These 'scripts' include the Bible readings, passage summaries, comprehension questions and ways to transition to prayer from the passage. Although these sample Bible reading sessions take the form of a script, they are not meant to be followed word for word. Rather, they are presented as models for what this *can* look like. The goal here is to help you envision how you can make times of Bible reading with your children come alive in a new and meaningful way.

These samples are generally intended for use with children aged 7-12. Will there be some 4, 5 and 6-year-olds who are ready for this kind of Bible reading? I think absolutely, yes. But for those younger children who are not yet ready, chapter 6 offers some general principles for *preparing* them for longer, more intensive times of reading the actual words of Scripture.

I hope that, by the end of this book, you will not only be convinced that you must joyfully begin this discipline with your kids, but you'll also be confident enough to get started (if you haven't already!).

6 Guidelines and principles for preparing younger children (aged 3-6)

As I stated earlier, it will be necessary for you, as parents, to use some discernment in terms of where your kids are in their understanding, development, and capacity to sit and listen to chunks of the Bible read to them. Generally, the samples that I provide in chapters 7 and 8 are going to be most helpful (and accessible) for children aged 7-12. Of course, if your 5-year-old is ready for this kind of engagement with the Bible in your estimation... you should go for it sooner rather than later! But for most kids between the ages of 3 and 6, here are a few tips for training them to listen to the Bible and engage with it for years to come.

Children's Bibles

Perhaps the most obvious place to start with children aged 3-6 is with solid children's Bibles that faithfully summarize and explain God's word in simple terms (with good pictures!). While there are many, many examples of these, I would strongly recommend finding a couple that help children to begin to put together the 'big story' of the Bible, rather than just picking out Bible stories. When Bible stories are isolated from that 'big picture' perspective they can seem somewhat random to children. *The Big Picture Story Bible* by David Helm (published by Crossway) and *The Jesus Storybook Bible* by Sally Lloyd-Jones (published by Zondervan) are just two examples of children's Bibles that seek to tell that 'big story'. We've used Helm's book for our kids, and it does a beautiful job of beginning to teach them—in very simple terms—the overarching story of God's creation and redemption of his fallen people, as well as the hope of final restoration in the new heavens and new earth. The great stories are there, of course, but they are a tool for helping very young children see that the Bible really is one big story about God's gracious redemption of his people... with Jesus Christ at the very centre of it.

Simpler translations and paraphrased Bibles

One step past children's Bibles would be translations or paraphrases of the Bible that are faithful, and yet utilize more 'every day' and easy-to-understand language for children. You might consider beginning to read some passages to your 5 and 6-year-old from the NIrV or the Good News Bible (of course being careful to check their accuracy against a more literal translation beforehand). We have to admit that if parts of the ESV Bible are difficult for us to understand... they're going to be hard for our young kids to understand too!

There are also good resources available for those who need a bit of help in knowing how to go about asking questions of younger kids as we read the Bible with them—for example, the *Table Talk* and *Beginning with God* series published by The Good Book Company.

Selections from the Bible

Finally, before you get to the stage of reading through entire books of the Bible, you can begin reading carefully chosen selections from the Bible to your children—even from essentially literal translations—that begin to acquaint them with important stories, key ideas, and gospel-centred themes of Scripture. For example, you could spend a few nights reading key stories from David's life, and begin talking about the importance of kingship, and the way that points ahead to Jesus. Then, you might read a couple of stories about Elijah and Elisha, and talk about the role of the prophets in the lives of God's people. From there, you could start to acquaint your children with the miracles and parables of Jesus. You see what I mean: short chunks, and selected stories can be a good precursor to reading through longer biblical books together.

Time to transition?

At some point (I'm suggesting at around age 7), your children will begin to ask questions about the Bible, salvation, the work of Jesus, etc. that go a bit beyond the simple explanations and narrations of typical children's Bibles. Or, they'll begin to have short children's Bibles essentially memorized! These can be indicators that they're getting ready to have Scripture read to them in longer chunks—that they're prepared for the next phase of Bible reading and discussion. And it's that next stage that I'll now describe and demonstrate for the remainder of the book.

7 Sample Bible reading plans (for children aged 7-12)

Genesis in three weeks

Here is a 'bare bones' reading schedule to use to move through the book of Genesis in three weeks with your children aged 7-12. This is a good representation of the way I moved through the book with my kids just a few months ago. On days when there is only one chapter listed, I would generally recommend reading the entire chapter word for word (unless there are some parts that need to have age-appropriate summaries). On days when there are two or three chapters listed, there is definitely some summary required, in order to cut down the total reading time. I've included more detailed explanation of this for Day 13 (Genesis 25-27), and in the example 'scripts' of our next chapter, you'll see in even more detail how I dealt with Day 17 (Genesis 38-39).

Day 1: read Genesis 1-2
Day 2: read Genesis 3
Day 3: read Genesis 4-5 (summarize chapter 5)
Day 4: read Genesis 6-7
Day 5: read Genesis 8-10
Day 6: read Genesis 11
Day 7: read Genesis 12

Skip Genesis 13-14

Day 8: read Genesis 15

Skip Genesis 16

Day 9: read Genesis 17
Day 10: read Genesis 18-19 (summarize some parts in age-appropriate ways)

Skip Genesis 20

Day 11: read Genesis 21-22

Skip Genesis 23

Day 12: read Genesis 24
Day 13: read Genesis 25-27

- Summarize 25:1-18 (Explain that Abraham died, and that he had many descendants, but the promise of God was going to come through Isaac.)
- Read 25:19-34
- Summarize 26:1-35 (Explain that Isaac was a lot like his father, Abraham; he sinned, and was dishonest about his wife, Rebekah.)

- Read 27:1-29
- Summarize 27:30-46 (Explain that Esau missed out on the blessing of Isaac, and that he hated Jacob, so Rebekah convinced Isaac to send Jacob away.)

Day 14: read Genesis 28-30
Day 15: read Genesis 31-33

Skip Genesis 34-36

Day 16: read Genesis 37
Day 17: read Genesis 38-39
Day 18: read Genesis 40-41
Day 19: read Genesis 42-44
Day 20: read Genesis 45-47
Day 21: read Genesis 48-50

1 Samuel in two weeks

As with the Genesis reading schedule, I'd recommend reading the entire chapter only when there is just one chapter listed for a particular day. But if there are two or three chapters listed, you'll need to be thoughtful and strategic about what parts to read, and what parts to summarize. On Day 1, for example, I read all of 1 Samuel 1 to my kids, and the second half of chapter two (I summarized Hannah's prayer, rather than reading all of it word for word). I give a more detailed example below of how you might decide to read and summarize 1 Samuel 18-20.

Day 1: read 1 Samuel 1-2
Day 2: read 1 Samuel 3

Day 3: read 1 Samuel 4-5

Skip 1 Samuel 6-7

Day 4: read 1 Samuel 8
Day 5: read 1 Samuel 9-11

Skip 1 Samuel 12

Day 6: read 1 Samuel 13
Day 7: read 1 Samuel 14
Day 8: read 1 Samuel 15
Day 9: read 1 Samuel 16-17
Day 10: read 1 Samuel 18-20

- Read 18:1-16
- Summarize 18:17-30 (Explain that David married Saul's daughter, and that no matter what Saul did, God gave David more and more success.)
- Read 19:1-10
- Summarize 19:11-24 (Explain that Saul kept trying to kill David, but that Michal, Saul's daughter and David's wife, helped him get away.)
- Read 20:1-17
- Summarize 20:18-42 (Explain that Jonathan found out that Saul really did want to kill David; he warned him, and they promised to be faithful friends forever.)

Skip 1 Samuel 21

Day 11: read 1 Samuel 22

Skip 1 Samuel 23

Day 12: read 1 Samuel 24

Day 13: read 1 Samuel 25

Skip 1 Samuel 26-27, 29-30

Day 14: read 1 Samuel 28 and 31

John's Gospel in two weeks

Since John is shorter, we were able to get through it in two weeks, with most days having only one chapter of text. As with Genesis and 1 Samuel, I did some summarizing on those days that did include two full chapters. For example, I read John 5:1-18, but summarized John 5:19-47 (which are all words of Jesus, focused on his authority, and the witnesses to his identity and authority).

The particular challenge of reading the Gospel of John with young children is that it contains long sections of monologue from Jesus—especially in chapters 14-17. For example, with the 'High Priestly Prayer' in John 17, it is very important to read the actual words, but also to stop often to make sure your children understand what Jesus is praying about at any given point.

Day 1: read John 1
Day 2: read John 2
Day 3: read John 3
Day 4: read John 4-5
Day 5: read John 6

Skip John 7-8

Day 6: read John 9-10
Day 7: read John 11

Day 8: read John 12
Day 9: read John 13
Day 10: read John 14-16:4a

Skip John 16:4b-33

Day 11: read John 17
Day 12: read John 18-19
Day 13: read John 20
Day 14: read John 21

8 Sample Bible reading sessions (for children aged 7-12)

As I said earlier, these 'scripts' are not necessarily meant to be used as such; instead they are intended to be examples of what reading a particular passage with your child *can* look like. My hope is that they give you some ideas to use (and adapt as necessary) with your own children in your own context.

Genesis 38-39

I've chosen to give you this example 'script' because it covers a part of the Bible that is really difficult to read with kids—in particular, Genesis 38 addresses the tricky issues of prostitution and incest. Below, you'll find a proposed model for how to engage with this chapter without either ignoring it completely, or forcing yourself to try to explain prostitution to a 7-year-old. Hopefully you'll see the importance of reading through books of the Bible sequentially, so that you can intentionally set the broader context for your children as you read. Take note of the way I connect Genesis 38 to both chapters 37 and 39, and choose between doing a word for word reading of some parts of the chapters and general summaries of others. This can be a helpful model for the way you approach the more difficult parts of the Bible with your 7 to 12-year-old children in the course of your daily Bible reading with them.

NB. In the 'scripts' below, wherever I give a summary of a Bible passage, I have also included that passage in full immediately afterwards. This is for your reference, so you can more easily see what text is being summarized.

Introductory comments and questions

Let's take a minute and remember what we read together yesterday. We started a new part of the story of Genesis, and we began to learn about the sons of Jacob (the grandson of Abraham). He had 12 sons, but he had a problem, right? Why did all of his sons not get along? ("Because Jacob had a favourite son, Joseph.") How did Joseph's brothers respond? What did they do? ("They were very jealous of Joseph; they hated him, and they threw him into a pit, and then sold him as a slave, and Joseph was taken to Egypt.") So where did we end the story last night? Where was Joseph, and what had happened to him? ("He was a slave in Egypt, working for a man named Potiphar.")

Summarize Genesis 38

Well, before we find out what happens to Joseph in Egypt, the writer of the book of Genesis does something really surprising. He actually takes us *back* to the land of Canaan, which is where Joseph was *before* he was taken away as a slave. We ended chapter 37 with Joseph in Egypt... chapter 39 will start with Joseph in Egypt. But in the middle, chapter 38 is all about Joseph's brother Judah who is still in Canaan. Here's what happens.

Judah, one of Joseph's older brothers, is back home in Canaan, after Joseph has been taken away to Egypt. Judah has sons who are very wicked, and don't listen to God at all. God actually punishes them by putting them to death. Judah's son's wife, Tamar, is left all alone, and Judah does not take care of her like he should. She does not obey God perfectly either; she lies, and pretends to be someone else. Judah is far worse than Tamar, though; he is angry at Tamar, and almost punishes her, even though he had sinned in much worse ways than she had. This part of the Bible story is full of sadness, sin, and messiness. Judah is not a slave in a foreign land like his brother Joseph (a "foreign land" is somewhere far away that is not your home). But Judah is actually still a slave, even though he is at home in his own land. He is a slave in a different way—he is a slave to *sin*. He is a slave to sin because he is doing the wrong thing and not living for God, and he makes a big mess because of it.

[The passage you are summarizing...] It happened at that time that Judah went down from his brothers and turned aside to a certain Adullamite, whose name was Hirah. There Judah saw the daughter of a certain Canaanite whose name was Shua. He took her and went in to her, and she conceived and bore a son, and he called his name Er. She conceived again and bore a son, and she called his name Onan. Yet again she bore a son, and she called his name Shelah. Judah was in Chezib when she bore him.

And Judah took a wife for Er his firstborn, and her name was Tamar. But Er, Judah's firstborn, was wicked in the sight of the LORD, and the LORD put him to death. Then Judah said to Onan, "Go in to your brother's wife and perform the duty of a brother-in-law to her, and raise up offspring for your brother." But Onan knew that the offspring would not be his. So whenever he went in to his brother's wife he would waste the semen on the ground, so as not to give offspring to his brother. And what he did was wicked in the sight of the LORD, and he put him to death also. Then Judah said to Tamar his daughter-in-law, "Remain a widow in your father's house, till Shelah my son grows up"— for he feared that he would die, like his brothers. So Tamar went and remained in her father's house.

In the course of time the wife of Judah, Shua's daughter, died. When Judah was comforted, he went up to Timnah to his sheepshearers, he and his friend Hirah the Adullamite. And when Tamar was told, "Your father-in-law is going up to Timnah to shear his sheep," she took off her widow's garments and covered herself with a veil, wrapping herself up, and sat at the entrance to Enaim, which is on the road to Timnah. For she saw that Shelah was grown up, and she had not been given to him in marriage. When Judah saw her, he thought she was a prostitute, for she had covered her face. He turned to her at the roadside and said, "Come, let me come in to you," for he did not know that she was his daughter-in-law. She said, "What will you give me, that you may come in to me?" He answered, "I will send you a young goat from the flock." And she said, "If you give me a pledge, until you send it—" He said, "What pledge shall I give you?" She replied, "Your signet and your cord and your staff that is in your hand." So he gave them to her and went in to her, and she conceived by him. Then she arose and went away, and taking off her veil she put on the garments of her widowhood.

When Judah sent the young goat by his friend the Adullamite to take back the pledge from the woman's hand, he did not find her. And he asked the men of the place, "Where is the cult prostitute who was at Enaim at the roadside?" And they said, "No cult prostitute has been here." So he returned to Judah and said, "I have not found her. Also, the men of the place said, 'No cult prostitute has been here.'" And Judah replied, "Let her keep the things as her own, or we shall be laughed at. You see, I sent this young goat, and you did not find her." About three months later Judah was told, "Tamar your daughter-in-law has been immoral. Moreover, she is pregnant by immorality." And Judah said, "Bring her out, and let her be burned." As she was being brought out, she sent word to her father-in-law, "By the man to whom these belong, I am pregnant." And she said, "Please identify whose these are, the signet and the cord and the staff." Then Judah identified them and said, "She is more righteous than I, since I did not give her to my son Shelah." And he did not know her again.

When the time of her labour came, there were twins in her womb. And when she was in labour, one put out a hand, and the midwife took and tied a scarlet thread on his hand, saying, "This one came out first." But as he drew back his hand, behold, his brother came out. And she said, "What a breach you have made for yourself!" Therefore his name was called Perez. Afterward his brother came out with the scarlet thread on his hand, and his name was called Zerah.

Stop to ask questions

So, who is Judah again? And where is he living, while Joseph has been sent away as a slave to Egypt? ("Judah is Joseph's older brother. He is living at home back in Canaan.") How does he sin, and not pay attention to God or his word? ("He did not take care of his son's wife

Tamar after his son died, and he tried to punish her, even though he had sinned in worse ways than she had.")

Introduce Genesis 39

So now, after looking back to Judah at home, we fly to Egypt, where Joseph has been taken as a slave. Back home in Canaan, Judah is a slave to his sin, and is obviously far from God. Let's see what is going on with Joseph, who is a slave in Egypt.

Read verses 1-6a

> Now Joseph had been brought down to Egypt, and Potiphar, an officer of Pharaoh, the captain of the guard, an Egyptian, had bought him from the Ishmaelites who had brought him down there. The LORD was with Joseph, and he became a successful man, and he was in the house of his Egyptian master. His master saw that the LORD was with him and that the LORD caused all that he did to succeed in his hands. So Joseph found favour in his sight and attended him, and he made him overseer of his house and put him in charge of all that he had. From the time that he made him overseer in his house and over all that he had, the LORD blessed the Egyptian's house for Joseph's sake; the blessing of the LORD was on all that he had, in house and field. So he left all that he had in Joseph's charge, and because of him he had no concern about anything but the food he ate. (vv. 1-6a)

Stop to ask questions

So, Joseph is a slave in Egypt, working for Potiphar. But how is God taking care of him there? ("God is helping him succeed in everything! Potiphar loves him and trusts him, and puts him as second in command over all his house.") How is this different from what is going on with Joseph's brother Judah, back at home? ("Judah is at home, but he is far from God; Joseph is in a foreign land, but God is very near to him.") But something very unfair is about to happen to Joseph...

Summarize verses 6b-20

Even though things had been going very well for Joseph in Egypt, something very unfair happens to him: Potiphar's wife accuses him of trying to attack her, even though he didn't do anything like that. Potiphar believes his wife, and takes her side, even though Joseph has done nothing wrong, and Joseph is thrown into prison in Egypt. Can you imagine that? First, he was a slave far from home. Just when his situation was getting better, now he is accused of a bad thing that he didn't even do... and he ends up in jail!

> *[The passage you are summarizing...]* Now Joseph was handsome in form and appearance. And after a time his master's wife cast her eyes on Joseph and said, "Lie with me." But he refused and said to his master's wife, "Behold, because of me my master has no concern about anything in the house, and he has put everything that he has in my charge. He is not greater in this house than I

am, nor has he kept back anything from me except you, because you are his wife. How then can I do this great wickedness and sin against God?" And as she spoke to Joseph day after day, he would not listen to her, to lie beside her or to be with her.

But one day, when he went into the house to do his work and none of the men of the house was there in the house, she caught him by his garment, saying, "Lie with me." But he left his garment in her hand and fled and got out of the house. And as soon as she saw that he had left his garment in her hand and had fled out of the house, she called to the men of her household and said to them, "See, he has brought among us a Hebrew to laugh at us. He came in to me to lie with me, and I cried out with a loud voice. And as soon as he heard that I lifted up my voice and cried out, he left his garment beside me and fled and got out of the house." Then she laid up his garment by her until his master came home, and she told him the same story, saying, "The Hebrew servant, whom you have brought among us, came in to me to laugh at me. But as soon as I lifted up my voice and cried, he left his garment beside me and fled out of the house."

As soon as his master heard the words that his wife spoke to him, "This is the way your servant treated me," his anger was kindled. And Joseph's master took him and put him into the prison, the place where the king's prisoners were confined, and he was there in prison." (vv. 6b-20)

Stop to ask questions

How might you feel if you were Joseph? What do you think will happen to Joseph? How has God taken care of him so far? Well, let's see what happens to him next.

Read verses 21-23

> But the LORD was with Joseph and showed him steadfast love and gave him favour in the sight of the keeper of the prison. And the keeper of the prison put Joseph in charge of all the prisoners who were in the prison. Whatever was done there, he was the one who did it. The keeper of the prison paid no attention to anything that was in Joseph's charge, because the LORD was with him. And whatever he did, the LORD made it succeed. (vv. 21-23)

Stop to ask questions

How did God take care of Joseph, even after he was blamed for something he didn't do, and thrown into jail in Egypt? ("Even in prison, God takes care of Joseph, and he becomes second in command of everything in the jail.")

Ask summary questions for follow-up discussion

How is what is happening with Joseph very different from what is happening with his brother Judah? ("Even though Joseph is far from home, he is close to God, and God is taking care of him. Judah is safe at home, but he is far from God, and is making a mess of his life.") That's right; even though things are difficult for Joseph, he continues to follow God's way. What in the story tells us what God is thinking? How do we know that he is pleased with Joseph? ("God is taking care of him, even in the hard things—even though Joseph is a slave, he becomes second in command of Potiphar's house. And then even when he's in jail, God takes care of him and he becomes second in command of the prison.")

Connect to Jesus

Can you think of an even greater example of someone who was in a really bad situation, but who was still more obedient to God than anyone else who has ever lived? It's Jesus. Think about it—Joseph was accused unfairly and thrown into jail; Jesus was accused unfairly and nailed to a cross. But God was in control; in fact, he used the worst thing that happened to Jesus to save us forever. We'll learn more about how God uses evil things to make his good plans come true as we keep on going in Joseph's story too.

Transition to prayer

Let's pray about this together. We've been learning that no matter our situation, or even if we get treated unfairly, the best place to be is near to God. Joseph doesn't stop trusting God, and God doesn't stop taking care of him, even when he is far from home.

Prayer

> Dear God, we want to love you, trust you, and obey you... even when we have to deal with hard things,

and even if we get treated unfairly. Help us to trust Jesus, your Son, and know that you are always with us wherever we go. Thank you that the best place to be is close to you, no matter what is happening around us! In Jesus' name. Amen.

1 Samuel 18

In reading this chapter with your children, I'm assuming that you've been making your way through chapters 1-17 of 1 Samuel, and have followed the developing story of the kingdom of Israel from there. You'll be able to tell from the 'script' below that the key points to bring out are based on the key characters who are prominent at this point in 1 Samuel. First, there's Saul—the 'people's choice' for king, who is now very much turning away from God towards pride and selfishness as he desperately tries to hold onto his power and position as king. Second, there is David—God's anointed king (1 Samuel 16), who is patiently waiting on God, even as he serves King Saul as a musician and soldier. Third, there is Jonathan—the one who, in this passage, gives us a beautiful example of the right response to God and God's chosen King. He supports David, loves him, and trusts God's plan for his life above his own personal interests. As you read this sample 'script' below, you should see that the major themes emerging from the passage are highlighted in the questions and prayer. Again, this is not meant to be something that you read word for word with your children, but rather a model of what one of these 10-15 minute Bible reading times could look like, as you read, teach, and 'pastor' your kids through God's word.

Introductory comments and questions

OK, do you remember what we read about last night? Who was the giant enemy of God and God's people, from the Philistines, who challenged God's people to battle?

("Goliath.") And what did David do? How did he defeat Goliath? ("He took only a sling and five stones into battle, and God helped him kill Goliath.") What did God's people do, once Goliath was dead, and the Philistines started running away? ("They all chased the Philistines out of the land of Israel.") Last question: What did we say about David? Who does he remind us of when he fights for God's people to be their King and Saviour? ("Jesus, who fought sin and death for us on the cross.")

Read verses 1-5

Now, we're going to continue on to the next chapter of 1 Samuel. We're going to be introduced to a new character: Jonathan, the son of Saul. Listen carefully as I read the first part of the story:

> As soon as he had finished speaking to Saul, the soul of Jonathan was knit to the soul of David, and Jonathan loved him as his own soul. And Saul took him that day and would not let him return to his father's house. Then Jonathan made a covenant with David, because he loved him as his own soul. And Jonathan stripped himself of the robe that was on him and gave it to David, and his armour, and even his sword and his bow and his belt. And David went out and was successful wherever Saul sent him, so that Saul set him over the men of war. And this was good in the sight of all the people and also in the sight of Saul's servants. (vv. 1-5)

Stop to explain and ask questions

Did you understand that part that I just read? Who is Jonathan? ("The son of Saul, the king.") How does he feel about David? ("He loves him; they are friends.") Why is that really surprising? What should have been next for Jonathan—the prince, and the son of the king? ("He should have been the next king.") What Jonathan does for David is amazing; he gives him his robe, his armour, and his sword and bow, telling him that he knows that he is God's choice for the next king. He's giving him the symbols of his kingship. So Jonathan is a pretty amazing guy, right? He's willing to give up his place as the next king, because he believes that God has chosen David, and he loves God even more than he loves the power of being king. What an amazing friend!

Read verses 6-7

OK, let's read a bit more...

> As they were coming home, when David returned from striking down the Philistine, the women came out of all the cities of Israel, singing and dancing, to meet King Saul, with tambourines, with songs of joy, and with musical instruments. And the women sang to one another as they celebrated,
>
> "Saul has struck down his thousands,
> and David his ten thousands." (vv. 6-7)

Stop to explain and ask questions

Do you see what the women of Israel are singing? They are saying that Saul destroyed lots of their enemies, but David has destroyed *even* more. Why would this song have bothered King Saul? ("They're saying that Saul is great, but that David is way better!")

Read verses 8-16

Let's keep reading...

> And Saul was very angry, and this saying displeased him. He said, "They have ascribed to David ten thousands, and to me they have ascribed thousands, and what more can he have but the kingdom?" And Saul eyed David from that day on.
>
> The next day a harmful spirit from God rushed upon Saul, and he raved within his house while David was playing the lyre, as he did day by day. Saul had his spear in his hand. And Saul hurled the spear, for he thought, "I will pin David to the wall." But David evaded him twice.
>
> Saul was afraid of David because the LORD was with him but had departed from Saul. So Saul removed him from his presence and made him a commander of a thousand. And he went out and came in before the people. And David had success in all his undertakings, for the LORD was with him. And when Saul saw that he had great success, he stood in fearful awe of him. But all Israel and Judah loved David, for he went out and came in before them. (vv. 8-16)

Stop to explain

Saul is pretty angry with David, right? In fact, he's the exact opposite of Jonathan, who loves God so much that he supports David and takes care of him, even though it means that Jonathan won't be king. Saul, though, is jealous of David. He is scared of David, especially when he sees that God is with David, and is helping him in everything he does. Saul even tries to kill David! But God takes care of him. David is God's chosen king, and God is going to make sure that his chosen king has success and safety in everything he does.

Summarize verses 17-30

Saul didn't just get mad at David. He also did more than throw a spear at him to try to kill him. Saul tried other ways to get rid of David. He tried sending him far away from Israel—into battle against the Philistines. He even tried using his own daughter to distract David, by giving her to David as his wife (Saul obviously didn't think very highly of his daughter!). But, in all of this, God continued to take care of David. David was God's chosen king, and he succeeded in battle, and no matter what Saul did, the people of Israel kept loving David more and more.

> *[The passage you are summarizing...]* Then Saul said to David, "Here is my elder daughter Merab. I will give her to you for a wife. Only be valiant for me and fight the LORD's battles." For Saul thought, "Let not my hand be against him, but let the hand of the Philistines be against him." And David said

to Saul, "Who am I, and who are my relatives, my father's clan in Israel, that I should be son-in-law to the king?" But at the time when Merab, Saul's daughter, should have been given to David, she was given to Adriel the Meholathite for a wife.

Now Saul's daughter Michal loved David. And they told Saul, and the thing pleased him. Saul thought, "Let me give her to him, that she may be a snare for him and that the hand of the Philistines may be against him." Therefore Saul said to David a second time, "You shall now be my son-in-law." And Saul commanded his servants, "Speak to David in private and say, 'Behold, the king has delight in you, and all his servants love you. Now then become the king's son-in-law.'" And Saul's servants spoke those words in the ears of David. And David said, "Does it seem to you a little thing to become the king's son-in-law, since I am a poor man and have no reputation?" And the servants of Saul told him, "Thus and so did David speak." Then Saul said, "Thus shall you say to David, 'The king desires no bride-price except a hundred foreskins of the Philistines, that he may be avenged of the king's enemies.'" Now Saul thought to make David fall by the hand of the Philistines. And when his servants told David these words, it pleased David well to be the king's son-in-law. Before the time had expired, David arose and went, along with his men, and killed two hundred of the Philistines. And David brought their foreskins, which were given in full number to

> the king, that he might become the king's son-in-law. And Saul gave him his daughter Michal for a wife. But when Saul saw and knew that the LORD was with David, and that Michal, Saul's daughter, loved him, Saul was even more afraid of David. So Saul was David's enemy continually.
>
> Then the commanders of the Philistines came out to battle, and as often as they came out David had more success than all the servants of Saul, so that his name was highly esteemed. (vv. 17-30)

Ask summary questions for follow-up discussion

What is it about Jonathan, Saul's son, that made him such an amazing friend to David? ("He loves him and supports him, even though it meant that he won't be the next king of Israel.") What can we learn from Jonathan? ("That it's more important to trust God and his plan than to chase what we want.") How does Saul feel about David, and how does he try to stop him? ("Saul hates David, envies him, and is scared of him. He tries to kill him, and tries to trick and trap him.") What is God's role in the story? What is he doing for David? ("He protects David, and makes sure that he succeeds in everything he does.") What do we learn about God, and his King, from this story? ("God is going to make sure his chosen king is safe, and succeeds in everything he does.")

Connect to Jesus

In the big story of the Bible, we're a long way from getting to the part where Jesus comes into the world. But this story of God's anointed King David points us ahead to Jesus the great King. God is going to make sure that Jesus' work for his people succeeds... no matter what. God wants us to be like Jonathan—supporting his chosen King (Jesus) in every way we can, even if it means giving up some things we really want.

Transition to prayer

So, what are some ways that we might talk back to God after reading this part of his word? How might we thank him? How might we ask him to help us? ("We can thank God for giving us a perfect King: Jesus, who is even better than King David! We can ask him to help us do whatever we can to serve and obey Jesus. We can try to give things—and give our lives—to Jesus, just like Jonathan did for David.")

Prayer

Dear God, we thank you that you show us in this story how you chose a good king for your people, and took care of him, and made everything he did succeed. Thank you that you protected David from King Saul, and that you helped Jonathan love and support him, even though it meant that he would never be king after his father Saul. God, we want to be like Jonathan. We want to support and follow your great chosen King: Jesus, your Son. Help us to obey him. Help us to follow him. Help us to be willing to give up things that we treasure to serve him better. In Jesus' name we pray. Amen.

John 3

I picked this chapter as a 'script' for this little book because it's an example of one that is filled predominantly with dialogue (and theologically heavy dialogue at that!). Most parents find that, in reading the Gospel of John to their children, they'll have an easier time with John 11 (the raising of Lazarus) than they will with John 3, or the theological prologue in John 1. In the 'model' Bible reading time below, note how I try to read the actual words of the passage, explaining along the way what is happening, and also helping my children see how what Jesus is saying connects to the bigger story of the Bible (the Old Testament prophets, etc.).

Introductory comments and questions

Do you remember what we read about last night, from John 2? What did Jesus do in the temple? ("He cleaned it out, because people had made it a place where they were selling things, instead of helping all kinds of people worship God.") Who might have not been happy about Jesus doing that? ("The religious leaders—the Pharisees.") Well, one of those Pharisees actually really liked Jesus; or, at least, he was very interested in learning more about him. But, he didn't want his friends to see him talking to Jesus because they might get angry at him! So this Pharisee decided to be sneaky. He would go and visit Jesus in the middle of the night... and ask him some questions.

Read verses 1-15

OK, let's read the first part of this passage together.

> Now there was a man of the Pharisees named Nicodemus, a ruler of the Jews. This man came to Jesus by night and said to him, "Rabbi, we know that you are a teacher come from God, for no-one can do these signs that you do unless God is with him." Jesus answered him, "Truly, truly, I say to you, unless one is born again he cannot see the kingdom of God." Nicodemus said to him, "How can a man be born when he is old? Can he enter a second time into his mother's womb and be born?" Jesus answered, "Truly, truly, I say to you, unless one is born of water and the Spirit, he cannot enter the kingdom of God. That which is born of the flesh is flesh, and that which is born of the Spirit is spirit. Do not marvel that I said to you, 'You must be born again.' The wind blows where it wishes, and you hear its sound, but you do not know where it comes from or where it goes. So it is with everyone who is born of the Spirit."
>
> Nicodemus said to him, "How can these things be?" Jesus answered him, "Are you the teacher of Israel and yet you do not understand these things? Truly, truly, I say to you, we speak of what we know, and bear witness to what we have seen, but you do not receive our testimony. If I have told you earthly things and you do not believe, how can you believe if I tell you heavenly things? No one has ascended into heaven except he who descended

from heaven, the Son of Man. And as Moses lifted up the serpent in the wilderness, so must the Son of Man be lifted up, that whoever believes in him may have eternal life. (vv. 1-15)

Stop to explain and ask questions

So, Nicodemus—this Pharisee—comes to Jesus at night to learn a little more about him. He may have thought that he could teach Jesus a few things, but Jesus ended up teaching *him* some things! What did Jesus say had to happen to a person for him or her to see God's kingdom? ("He said that you have to be 'born again'.") What did Nicodemus think he meant by that? ("That you had to actually become a baby in your mummy's tummy again!") Is that what Jesus was talking about? ("No.") It's a little bit confusing, but Jesus is talking about something happening inside of us; when we say "yes" to God—when we say sorry for our sins, and believe in Jesus—it's like we are really born for the first time, only this time not on the outside but on the *inside*! Jesus is saying that this kind of birth has to happen... even for Nicodemus, who is one of the top religious leaders of the Jews. This would have been very surprising to Nicodemus!

But, Jesus tells Nicodemus that this shouldn't have been so surprising to him. Do you remember the part where Jesus talks about the "wind" and the "flesh" and the "Spirit"? He is actually reminding Nicodemus of a part of the Old Testament—from the prophet Ezekiel. Ezekiel was a prophet who saw a vision (a picture from God, or perhaps a kind of dream given by God) of dead, dry bones coming to life. Jesus is telling Nicodemus that Ezekiel's vision of dead bones coming to life and being real people is a picture of what needs to happen inside Nicodemus. He can't just be in God's kingdom because he is a Jewish leader; he needs to come alive on the inside, by trusting God's Son!

There's another part of the Old Testament that Jesus talks to Nicodemus about. What character in the Old Testament did Jesus mention? ("Moses!") He reminds Nicodemus of that part of the Moses story in the book of Numbers, where the people are getting bitten by snakes because they sinned, and God tells Moses to make a bronze snake, and lift it up on a pole. Everyone who looks at the snake gets healed from their snakebites! Jesus is telling Nicodemus that this, too, was a picture that pointed to him. Jesus will be the one lifted up; everyone who believes in him will be saved... they will be "born again" inside.

Read verses 16-36

OK, let's read the rest of the chapter. At this point, John (the disciple of Jesus who wrote the Gospel of John) starts to talk again. He's done telling us about the conversation of Jesus with Nicodemus, and he wants to explain more about how *all* people can believe in Jesus, and be "born again" like Jesus explains to Nicodemus.

> "For God so loved the world, that he gave his only Son, that whoever believes in him should not perish but have eternal life. For God did not send his Son into the world to condemn the world, but

in order that the world might be saved through him. Whoever believes in him is not condemned, but whoever does not believe is condemned already, because he has not believed in the name of the only Son of God. And this is the judgement: the light has come into the world, and people loved the darkness rather than the light because their works were evil. For everyone who does wicked things hates the light and does not come to the light, lest his works should be exposed. But whoever does what is true comes to the light, so that it may be clearly seen that his works have been carried out in God."

After this Jesus and his disciples went into the Judean countryside, and he remained there with them and was baptizing. John also was baptizing at Aenon near Salim, because water was plentiful there, and people were coming and being baptized (for John had not yet been put in prison). Now a discussion arose between some of John's disciples and a Jew over purification. And they came to John and said to him, "Rabbi, he who was with you across the Jordan, to whom you bore witness—look, he is baptizing, and all are going to him." John answered, "A person cannot receive even one thing unless it is given him from heaven. You yourselves bear me witness, that I said, 'I am not the Christ, but I have been sent before him.' The one who has the bride is the bridegroom. The friend of the bridegroom, who stands and hears him, rejoices greatly at the bridegroom's voice. Therefore this joy of mine is now complete. He must increase, but I must decrease."

He who comes from above is above all. He who is of the earth belongs to the earth and speaks in an earthly way. He who comes from heaven is above all. He bears witness to what he has seen and heard, yet no-one receives his testimony. Whoever receives his testimony sets his seal to this, that God is true. For he whom God has sent utters the words of God, for he gives the Spirit without measure. The Father loves the Son and has given all things into his hand. Whoever believes in the Son has eternal life; whoever does not obey the Son shall not see life, but the wrath of God remains on him. (vv. 16-36)

Stop to explain and ask questions

What did John (the Gospel writer) say about God's love for the world? ("He loved the world by sending his Son to die.") How are people everywhere supposed to respond? ("Believe in him.") What seems to be bothering John the Baptist's followers about Jesus? ("They are upset because lots of people are leaving John... and starting to follow Jesus.") What does John tell them? ("Jesus will get greater and greater, and John the Baptist will become less and less.") John is explaining that his role is not to make himself look great, but to tell everyone how great Jesus is!

Connect to Jesus and ask summary questions[9]

This is an amazing chapter about Jesus! What are some things we learned about Jesus? What are some things we learned about people, and how they should respond to Jesus?

- Jesus wants people to be "born again"—to be made new inside, as they believe in him.
- Jesus is like the serpent that Moses held up for the Israelites; he will be lifted up, and all who look to him will be saved.
- Jesus died for sins on the cross, and this is to show God's love for the world.
- John the Baptist is a great example of our response to Jesus; we want others to follow him, and we should be OK with not being as important as Jesus!

Transition to prayer

Let's pray together about some of these things we learned from John 3 today. There are many ways that we can ask God to help us make Jesus look great through our words, actions, and decisions. And we need to always remember why Jesus is so wonderful; he is the Lord, God and Saviour. He died for our sins, so that by believing in him we might have life in God—we might be "born again" on the inside.

---

9 Because this passage is from the New Testament, the 'Connect to Jesus' and 'Summary' sections overlap more than in our examples from Genesis 38-39 and 1 Samuel 18.

Prayer

Father, thank you for this passage about Nicodemus, the Jewish leader who came to Jesus in secret at night. Thank you that Jesus explained so clearly to him, and to us, that we need to be "born again" by believing in you as the Son of God, and the Saviour who was lifted up on a cross to save sinners. Jesus, help us to believe in you! And, help us to want others to believe in you too, just like John the Baptist did. Amen.

Matthias Media is an evangelical publishing ministry that seeks to persuade all Christians of the truth of God's purposes in Jesus Christ as revealed in the Bible, and equip them with high-quality resources, so that by the work of the Holy Spirit they will:

- abandon their lives to the honour and service of Christ in daily holiness and decision-making
- pray constantly in Christ's name for the fruitfulness and growth of his gospel
- speak the Bible's life-changing word whenever and however they can—in the home, in the world and in the fellowship of his people.

Our resources range from Bible studies and books through to training courses, audio sermons and children's Sunday School material. To find out more, and to access samples and free downloads, visit our website:

www.matthiasmedia.com

How to buy our resources

1. Direct from us over the internet:
 – in the US: www.matthiasmedia.com
 – in Australia: www.matthiasmedia.com.au

2. Direct from us by phone: please visit our website for current phone contact information.

3. Through a range of outlets in various parts of the world. Visit **www.matthiasmedia.com/contact** for details about recommended retailers in your part of the world.

4. Trade enquiries can be addressed to:
 – in the US and Canada: sales@matthiasmedia.com
 – in Australia and the rest of the world: sales@matthiasmedia.com.au

Register at our website for our **free** regular email update to receive information about the latest new resources, **exclusive special offers**, and free articles to help you grow in your Christian life and ministry.

Fatherhood

What it is and what it's for

By Tony Payne

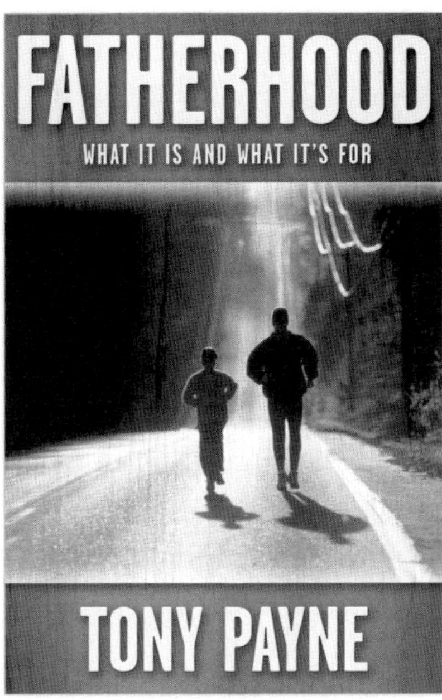

There are enough books about how to be a good father to fill a bloke's shed.

This book is different.

This book goes back to the drawing board—the Bible—and answers the question: what is a father anyway? And the answer will give dads a whole new way to think about their role and what they are trying to do.

But it's not a book of 'theory'. Drawing on his years of experience as a father of five, Tony Payne provides bucketloads of practical wisdom and advice.

Fatherhood is essential reading for all fathers, prospective fathers, and anyone who thinks fatherhood is important.